REALITY AND RELIGION
MEDITATIONS ON GOD, MAN AND NATURE

SADHU SUNDAR SINGH

Foreword by
B.H STREETER

FV ÉDITIONS

CONTENTS

PREFACE   v

INTRODUCTION   1
1. THE PURPOSE OF CREATION   8
2. THE INCARNATION   11
3. PRAYER   14
4. MEDITATION   21
5. THE FUTURE LIFE   27
6. THE NEW BIRTH   29
7. LOVE   32
8. THOUGHT AND SENSE   35
9. PHILOSOPHY AND INTUITION   38
10. PERFECTION   41
11. REAL PROGRESS AND SUCCESS   44
12. THE CROSS   46
13. FREE WILL   50
14. RULES OF HEALTH   53
15. CONSCIENCE   55
16. THE WORSHIP OF GOD   57
17. THE SEARCH AFTER REALITY   60

18. REPENTANCE AND
    SALVATION   65
19. ORIGINAL SIN   69
20. THE VEDANTA AND
    PANTHEISM   72
21. CHRIST OUR REFUGE   74
22. ENEMIES BIG AND SMALL   77
23. "STRANGERS AND
    PILGRIMS ON THE EARTH"   81
24. FAITH AND PURITY   84
25. REVELATIONS OF CHRIST   86
26. HUMILITY   89
27. TIME AND ETERNITY   91

PREFACE

In this little book I have put down some of the ideas and illustrations which are the outcome of my meditation. I am neither a philosopher nor a theologian, but a humble servant of the Lord, whose delight it is to meditate on the love of God and on the great wonders of His creation. It is impossible to describe all that I know and feel about Reality through my internal senses in meditation and prayer. Words cannot express all the deep truths which the soul feels in these solemn moments. Such truths though unspoken are readily and easily understood by receptive minds. Words, in fact, may lead more to misunderstanding than to real understanding.

I am unable, I repeat, to express all my deep feelings and thoughts, but I shall try to write down at least some of them as well as I can. Should readers be helped even a little by this attempt, I shall try later to explain my other ideas and experiences which at present I hesitate, for various reasons, to place before the public.

I would like to acknowledge here the great help I have received from Dr. A. J. Appasamy, M.A. (Harvard) and D.Phil. (Oxon.), in translating this book from Urdu into English. My thanks are also due to Rev. R. W. Pelly, Bishop's College, Calcutta, for reading through the manuscript and suggesting many valuable corrections.

SUNDAR SINGH
Sabathu, Simla Hills September 1923.

INTRODUCTION

"What has the Sadhu been doing since ?" That, I imagine, is the question which will be asked by many of those whose imagination, four years ago, was kindled by the parables, the personality — or even by a distant glimpse of the saffron robe — of the notable Indian Sadhu Sundar Singh, He left England in May 1920 to address a series of meetings that had been arranged for him in America and Australia, returning to India in September. The Christians at Colombo and at Bombay, his port of landing in India, had made great preparations to celebrate his " conquest of the West " with a public ovation. Naturally, this was not to the Sadhu's taste, and he caused no small disappointment and some resentment by declining to be made a hero. He avoided the crowds, and at once went North. The following summer he returned to the risks and hardships of mission work in Thibet. The anecdote that follows, abridged from an Indian newspaper, will illustrate the life he led.

One day in a lonely mountain spot a company of brigands set upon the Sadhu, stripped him, and, apparently, were about to despatch him. Impressed, however, by his demeanour, they hesitated. The Sadhu took advantage of the respite to begin a simple religious address. Still more impressed, they restored his clothing and conducted him to their cave, signifying their willingness to hear more. After a while they produced some rough food and invited him to share it. A bowl was handed him into which some milk was to be poured. As it was extremely dirty, the Sadhu began to wipe it out, before holding it out to be filled. At once the leader of the band, with an air of attentive consideration, took it from him, scoured it out with his own tongue and returned it, with a polite gesture, to the Sadhu. In the matter of drinking-vessels the high-caste Indian is far more sensitive even than the most delicate of European ladies; each member of a family has his own cup, which is never used by any other. But the Sadhu, appreciating the courtesy of the intention, accepted the kindly service in the spirit in which it was meant; and went on with his discourse and his meal.

In 1922 he accepted a reiterated invitation to visit Switzerland and Sweden. On his way to Europe he was enabled to realise his life's dream and visit the sacred sites of Palestine as the guest of Sir William Willcocks, noted as the originator of the great Assouan Dam, whose interest in him (it is a matter of satisfaction to me to reflect) had been aroused by reading the book The Sadhu by Dr. A. J. Appasamy and myself. From Switzerland, where he was received with great enthusiasm, the Sadhu went to Sweden, spending a fortnight in Germany en route. In Sweden he was the guest of Archbishop Soderblom of Upsala, who had organised a kind of Mission for him to conduct, and who subsequently published a scientific study on the subject of his mystical experience. Indeed, on the Continent a considerable literature about the Sadhu has come into existence — in French, German, and the Scandinavian languages. The Sadhu spent a short time in Denmark and (I think) Norway, and also visited Holland. He then came to England, but was so exhausted by his labours that he was compelled to rest. He, however, managed to address the Keswick Convention and a meeting in Wales before returning to India. Last summer a false report that he had been murdered in Thibet appeared in many newspapers, both in England and on the Continent. The death of his father had recently taken place, and it is supposed that similarity of names had given rise to the rumour.

Of the origin of the present volume I cannot do better than quote the account given me in a letter by Dr. Appasamy: " The Sadhu wrote to me to join him at Sabathu and work with him at his new book. Sabathu is about two or three hours' railway journey from Simla. It is a military station, and is three or four thousand feet above sea-level. His father insisted on buying a house here where his son could retire for rest, meditation, and study. Instead of buying a bungalow, as suggested by his father, the Sadhu has bought a large though old Mission-house, for Rs.roo.

You go through the dirtiest and busiest part of the town to get to this house. His next-door neighbours belong to the ' sweeper ' (i.e. scavenger) class, who often in the quiet of the night indulge in weird music or noisy quarrels. As, however, the house is on the edge of the town, you get, out on the other side, a magnificent view of the hills, extending for miles.

I think the house is a symbol of the two worlds with which the Sadhu constantly tries to live in contact — the busy world of men, sometimes dirty and sordid, and the world of nature so beautiful and calm. "The house is occupied by a friend of his, a doctor working in the Leper Asylum at Sabathu. The Sadhu comes up here whenever he feels the need for quiet work and study or rest. He has a room where he treasures the photographs of his friends and others whom he has met in the course of his travels, and where he also keeps a few books! Among these books I noticed two volumes of an Outline of Science recently edited by Prof. J. A. Thomson: the Sadhu has read through these two volumes carefully. The doctor, with whom the Sadhu stays when he comes up, is a married man and has four children. I was often interested in observing the Sadhu talking or playing with the children. People sometimes say the Sadhu ought to found a Monastery of some sort and train up other Sadhus. I think he would be very unhappy in such an environment. Though an ' ascetic ' he is really a lover of family life, and feels most happy in a home. "The Sadhu had the manuscript of Reality and Religion completed in Urdu. He said he had worked about twelve hours a day at it for twelve days. He kept the manuscript in his hand and gave the substance of each paragraph in English. Sometimes I took word for word what he said, and sometimes I put down the substance of his paragraphs, using, wherever possible, his own language." When I read the book in MS., what struck me was the clarity of the exposition. Ideas about God, Man, and Nature which most of us find it difficult to convey even to people of trained intelligence, are here expressed in a way which would be readily comprehensible to the simplest minds. As such it cannot fail, I think, to find a welcome from a wide circle of readers. Here and there are sentences to which a philosopher or scientist might take exception; but, as the Sadhu makes no pretence to be either of these, the discerning reader will not cavil at details, but will prefer rather to appreciate the direct simplicity of religious insight which pervades the whole.

B. H. STREETER. Queen's College, Oxford,
February 6, 1924.

1
THE PURPOSE OF CREATION

> *"In the beginning was the Word,*
> *and the Word was with God,*
> *and the Word was God. . . .*
> *All things were made*
> *through Him, and without*
> *Him was not anything made*
> *"*
>
> — JOHN 1:1, 1:3

The Eternal Word (Logos) existed before all Time and before the creation of the Universe. Through Him all things, animate and inanimate, came into existence. It is impossible for lifeless things to come into being of themselves or to produce living beings, as life alone produces life, and the source of all life is God. By His creative power, God brought all inanimate things into existence. Into these He infused life, and into man, the highest among created beings, He " breathed the breath of life and he became a living soul." " God created man in His own image and likeness, and gave him dominion over all the earth."

1. God's purpose in creation is not to complete any lack in His Being, for He is perfect in Himself, But He creates because it is in His nature to create. He gives life, as the impartation of life is of the very essence of His life-giving power and activity. And to make men happy by His creation and to give them real joy by His life-giving presence is of the very essence of His love. The happiness we derive from creation has its limits. God alone can completely meet the needs of human hearts and satisfy them in perfection. If men are without this joy, it is the result of their igno-

rance or disobedience and rebellion against God.

2. Beings, in worlds seen and unseen, are numberless. Through these numberless species are revealed God's numberless attributes. Each species, according to its own capacity, reflects some aspect of God's nature. Even through sinners His Fatherly love is revealed, as He gives them an opportunity to repent and to have the eternal life of peace and joy in Him.

2
THE INCARNATION

A child may read the word "God" merely as a word, without thinking anything of the Truth behind it. But as his mind matures, he begins to think and understand something at least of the meaning of the word. Just so the beginner in the spiritual life, however learned he may be, may think of Christ, the Word incarnate, as a great man or even as a prophet, but he does not go further in his estimate of Him. But as he grows in spiritual experience and enjoys His presence, then he begins to realise the fact that Christ is God incarnate in whom " dwelleth all the fullness of the Godhead bodily" (Col. ii. 9). "In Him was life, and the life was the light of men " (John i. 4).

2. A man cannot give adequate expression to his personality through words, though sometimes he may even coin new words to express his ideas, nor through symbols and illustrations. The body also is unable to set forth all the qualities and powers of the soul which constitute personality. In other words, much in human personality lies hidden while man is in this world, only a part being revealed. A spiritual being can fully express itself only in a spiritual world, when all conditions, external as well as internal, meet his needs and help his progress.

If this is true of a human spirit, how impossible it is for the eternal Word to reveal His Godhead adequately through a body! He revealed Himself as much as it was possible and necessary for man's salvation. But His real glory will be manifested in its fullness in heaven only.

3. The question may arise: How can we believe in Reality without seeing and knowing it

fully? A full knowledge of Reality, I may point out here, is not necessary to make us believe in Reality. For instance, some organs of the body, on which our life depends so much, remain hidden from our eyes. No one has ever seen his own brain or heart, and yet no one ever denies that he has them. When we are thus unable to see our own brain and heart, on which our life depends largely, how much more difficult must it be to see the Creator of our brain and heart, on whom all our life depends!

3
PRAYER

There are some plants whose leaves and flowers fold themselves when the Sun goes down, and unfold again when softly touched on the morrow by the Sun's light. In this way do they absorb the warmth and life of the Sun, so necessary for their growth and existence. Just so in prayer our hearts are open to the Sun of Righteousness, and we are safe from the dangers and difficulties of darkness and grow into the fullness of the stature of Christ.

2. By prayer we cannot change God's plans, as some people seem to think. But the man who prays is himself changed. The capacities

of the soul, which are imperfect in this imperfect life, are daily reaching towards perfection.

A bird sits brooding over her eggs. At first, in the eggs, there is only a kind of liquid without form or shape. But as the mother continues to sit on them, the unformed matter in the eggs becomes changed into the form of the mother. The change is not in the mother but in the eggs. So, when we pray, God is not changed but we are changed into His glorious image and likeness.

3. Vapour rises from the earth generated by the Sun's heat. Defying, as it were, the law of gravity, it goes up into the air and then comes down as rain and makes the earth fruitful. Our real prayers likewise, kindled by the fire of the Holy Ghost, rise up to God, overcoming sin and evil, and come back to the earth filled with His blessings.

4. Ctenophores or sea gooseberries are so extremely delicate that the splash of a wave would tear them into shreds. Whenever there is even a hint of an approaching storm, they sink deep into the sea, beyond the reach of the

storm and away from the waves. Just so, when the man of prayer anticipates Satan's attacks and the storm of sin and suffering in the world, at once he dives down into the ocean of God's love where there is eternal peace and calm.

5, A philosopher went to see a mystic. They were sitting together in silence for some time. Then said the mystic to the philosopher as he was about to go away, " I feel all you think." And the philosopher said, " I cannot even think all that you feel." It is clear that earthly wisdom is unable to feel and understand Reality. Only those who commune with God in prayer can really know Reality.

6. The wonderful peace which the man of prayer feels while praying is not the result of his own imagination or thought, but is the outcome of the presence of God in the soul. The vapour rising from a pond cannot become large clouds and come down as rain. It is only from the mighty ocean that such large clouds, filled with the rain that quenches the thirsty earth and makes it fertile, can take their rise. It is not from our subconscious minds but from the il-

limitable ocean of God's love, with which we are in contact in prayer, that the peace comes.

7. The Sun burns perpetual noon. The change of day and night and the movement of the seasons are not due to the Sun but to the rotation of the earth. Just so the Sun of Righteousness is " the same yesterday, and to-day, and for ever " (Heb. xiii. 8). If we are exalted with joy or sunk in gloom, it is owing to our position towards Him. When we open our hearts to Him in meditation and prayer, the rays of the Sun of Righteousness will heal the wounds of our sins and give us perfect health (Mai. iv. 2).

8. The laws of nature are the appointed means by which God works in man and other creatures for their progress and benefit. Miracles are not against the laws of nature. There are higher laws of nature which we do not ordinarily know. Miracles are in accordance with those higher laws. In prayer we come to know gradually these higher laws.

The highest miracle is the filling of our souls with peace and joy. We may think that such peace is impossible in a world of sin and suffering. But the impossible becomes possible. Apples do not grow in hot countries nor mangoes in snowy lands. If they did, we might speak of such occurrence as a miracle. Tropical plants do, however, grow in cold countries if the conditions are prepared for them.

9. If all men had the receptive spirit and the ready ear and could hear the voice of God speaking to them, it would not be necessary for Evangelists and Prophets to go about proclaiming the will of God. But all men are not so receptive. Hence the necessity for preachers of the Word. But sometimes more good can be done by praying than by preaching. A man praying intently in a cave can help men considerably by his prayer. Influences issue from him and spread all round effectively, though silently, just as wireless messages are communicated by invisible means, and just as the words we speak are conveyed by mysterious vibrations to others.

10. Sometimes green and fruitful trees are found standing on dry land, where there is not

much rain. On careful examination, it has been found that these trees are fresh and green, bearing fruit, because their hidden roots touch hidden streams of water running through the earth. We may be surprised when we see men of prayer, full of peace, radiant with joy and leading fruitful lives amidst the misery and sin of this world. It is because by prayer the hidden roots of their faith reach down to the Source of Living Water and draw from it energy and life and bring forth fruits unto life eternal (Psalm i. 2, 3).

11. The tips of the roots of trees are so sensitive that, almost as if by instinct, they turn away from spots where there is no nourishment and spread themselves in places where they can gather sap and life. Men of prayer have also this power of discernment. By unerring intuition, they turn away from fraud and illusion and find the Reality on which all life depends.

12. Men who do not hold converse with God in prayer are not worthy to be called men. They are like trained animals who can do cer-

tain things in certain ways at certain times. Sometimes they are even worse than animals, because they do not realise their nothingness in themselves, their relation to God and their duties to God and man. But men of prayer attain the right to become sons of God and are moulded by Him after His own image and likeness.

4
MEDITATION

The brain is a very subtle and sensitive instrument, furnished with many fine senses which, in meditation, receive messages from the unseen world and stimulate ideas far above normal human thought. The brain does not produce these ideas, but receives them from the spiritual, invisible world above and interprets them in terms of the conditions and circumstances familiar to men. Some people receive such messages in dreams; others in visions; and yet others during waking hours in meditation. Prayer enables us to distinguish between the useful and the useless among messages thus received, because in real prayer, light streams out from God and illumines the innermost, sensitive part of the soul, which is the conscience or the moral sense. Rich colours, fine music, and other wonderful sights and sounds from the invisible world are reflected in the inner part of the brain. Poets and painters, often without understanding their real source, try to interpret in their poems and paintings these invisible realities impinging upon them. But the man of meditation touches the heart, as it were, of such realities and enjoys their bliss, as his soul and the spiritual world, from which they come, are closely akin.

2. Sometimes when visiting new places we feel as if we have been already there or as if we have some unknown connection with them. For this, three explanations may be offered. First, some one else who had visited the places may have thought about them and, without our knowledge, communicated his ideas to us in a mysterious way. Secondly, we may have seen other places like them, and the memory of the similarity may have appeared to our minds in a

new form. Or thirdly, a reflection of the unseen world may have fallen on our minds, because our souls are connected with that world, and often, without our knowledge, we are being influenced by impressions from that world. This world is a copy of the invisible world — in other words, the manifestation of the spiritual world in a material form. Our thoughts are being constantly affected by the resemblance between the two worlds. When we spend enough time in meditation, this connection between the two worlds becomes more and more distinct and clear.

3. In meditation the real condition of the soul is revealed. While engaged thus, we are, in a sense, giving an opportunity to God to speak to us and to bless us with His richest blessings. Whatever we suppose, no thought, word, or deed is ever wiped out. But it is imprinted on our soul — in other words, recorded in " the book of Life." Meditation enables us to do everything in the fear and love of God and to keep clean the entries in the book of Life upon which our future bliss or pain depends.

4. God is infinite and we are finite. We cannot indeed fully understand the infinite God, but He has created in us a sense which enables us to enjoy Him. The ocean is vast and we cannot see all its immense expanse and know all about its great treasures. But with the mere tip of our tongue, we can feel at once that the ocean is salt. We have not come to know all that there is to know about the ocean, but we have found out, by our sense of taste, a most important fact about the nature of its water.

5. In fear, anger or madness, men do extraordinary things, breaking even iron chains. This strength is apparently inherent in man but finds expression only when the whole of his energy is directed towards one end. Likewise in meditation man's strength, reinforced by divine power, can break the bondage of sin and do great and useful work. At the same time, this God-given power, if used in wrong ways, may prove dangerous. Bombs, machine-guns, cannon — how mighty they are, and yet how destructive and dangerous!

6. When absorbed in thought we do not,

even though we are fully conscious, notice the fragrance of flowers, the charm of music or the beauty of nature. They seem to have no existence for us. Just so, to people absorbed in worldly things, spiritual realities do not seem to exist. Seeing they see not, hearing they hear not (Matt. xiii. 13).

7. One day I saw a flower and began to think about its fragrance and its beauty. As I thought more deeply, I saw the Creator behind His creation, though hidden from my gaze. This filled me with joy. But my joy was greater still when I found Him working in my own soul. I was led to exclaim: " Oh! How wonderful Thou art! Separate from Thy creation and yet ever filling it with Thy glorious Presence."

8. Christ did not write anything. Nor did He ask His apostles to write down His teaching. This is because, in the first place, His words are spirit and life. He knows that life can be infused only into life, not into the pages of a book. In the second place, other Teachers left behind books, because they were going away

from their disciples and they wanted to help them in times of need through their books, which took the place of their living voice. Our Lord, on the other hand, has never left His followers. He is with us always and His living Voice and Presence ever give us counsel. After His Ascension, the same indwelling Spirit inspired the disciples to write the Gospels.

9. If we repeat over and over again the same thought, word or deed, that becomes habit and habit makes character. Therefore, whatever we think or say or do, we must consider carefully what their consequences, good or bad, will be. We must not be indifferent about doing good, otherwise we shall be in danger of losing the capacity to do good. To do a thing well is difficult; to undo a wrong thing and to put it right is still more difficult; but to spoil a thing is altogether easy. It takes much time and trouble to grow a tree, but it is so easy to cut it down. When it is dry and dead, it is impossible to bring it to life again.

5
THE FUTURE LIFE

Belief in the future life has been found among all nations at all times. Desires imply a possible fulfilment. Thirst implies the existence of water, and hunger of food. The desire to live for ever is itself a proof of its fulfilment.

2. Again, we have some higher, nobler desires of the Spirit which cannot possibly be fulfilled in this world, Therefore there must be another spiritual world in which these desires can be met. This material world cannot by any means satisfy our spiritual cravings.

3. The soul's real desire can only be satis-

fied by God who has created the soul and the desire for Him inherent in it. Because God has created man in His own likeness, man has in him something of the Divine nature which longs for fellowship with Him. Like seeks like by the laws of being. And when we are rooted in the Eternal Being, we shall not only feel satisfied, but also have eternal Life in Him.

6
THE NEW BIRTH

It is an admitted fact that children inherit largely the character of their parents. They are also influenced by the environment, e.g. the habits of their parents and others with whom they are brought into constant contact. Children of bad parents, living in a bad environment, are sure to be bad. Every condition makes it impossible for them to be good. If such children turn out to be good, it will be a great miracle. We know that such miracles have taken place more or less everywhere. These miracles prove the existence of a great hidden Power which breaks fetters and sets men free from the bondage of sin and converts sinners into new creatures. This is the new birth. The great hidden Power is the Holy Ghost who works for the salvation of those who repent and believe in Christ.

2. There have been many criminals who, in spite of the severe punishment given them by their governments, have not been changed a whit. Neither has the love of their dear ones and friends nor their exhortation produced any effect upon them. All possible means have been used to reform them, but without avail. But sometimes when they have been led to Christ, they have been entirely changed in a moment and become new men. Then those who were selfish and living in sin were transformed in their lives and began to help and serve others. Formerly they persecuted and killed others; now they themselves are ready to be persecuted and killed for others. This is to be born again. Is this not proof enough that Christ is the Saviour of men, that He is the

Great Physician who diagnoses correctly men's diseases and heals them? Who else can heal the broken heart except He who is the Creator of the heart? Who else but He can change sinners into saints?

7
LOVE

God is the source of love. The force of gravity which keeps the worlds in space is, so to speak, the manifestation in matter of that spiritual force of gravity, which is love and whose source is God. A magnet attracts steel, not because steel is a valuable metal, but because steel has the capacity to respond. It does not attract gold. Gold may be more precious, but it is not responsive. God in like manner draws sinners, however sinful they may be, if they repent and respond to Him, and not others who are self-righteous and who do not yield to the sway of His love.

2. A kiss is the outward sign of a mother's love for her child. If the child has a contagious disease, the mother may refrain from kissing him, but her love for the suffering child is not less, but more, as he needs more of her care and love. Just so, God may seem outwardly to forsake those who have fallen a prey to the contagion of sin, but His love for them is infinitely more than a mother's love for her child (Isaiah xlix. 15). Like His other attributes, His patience also is infinite. Men, like small kettles, boil quickly with wrath at the least wrong. Not so God. If God were as wrathful, the world would have been a heap of ruins long ago.

3. If two men love the same person they become rivals and are jealous of each other. But this is not the case with man's love for God. A man who loves God is not jealous if others also love God, He is grieved if they do not love Him. The reason for this difference between man's love for man and man's love for God is that God's love is infinite. A man cannot respond with equal affection to all those who love him, as his capacity for love is limited ;

but God's capacity for love is without limit and, therefore, is sufficient for all.

4. Christ will live in us and our whole life will become like His. Salt, when dissolved in water, may disappear, but it does not cease to exist. We can be sure of its presence by tasting the water. Likewise, the indwelling Christ, though unseen, will be made evident to others from the love which He imparts to us.

8
THOUGHT AND SENSE

Thoughts are not only the impressions of outward things on our senses but are also our mind's responses to impressions coming to us through our senses. Thus the growth and the progress of mind towards the attainment of perfection depends on external as well as internal conditions. A tree may have life in itself, but before its leaves can unfold, its flowers blossom and its fruit ripen, it needs air and light and warmth. The tree, that is, depends upon certain external as well as internal conditions for its growth and maturity.

2. Through the outer senses we come to

know the outer world, and through the inner senses, the inner spiritual world. The rise of a thought about anything in the mind is a proof not only of the mind which thinks, but also of the existence of that thing. In other words, we might say that the thought is a reflection on our mind of that thing. Sometimes, even without intending to do so, we are led to think, which means that something outside is reflecting itself in our minds. Where there is fragrance, there must be flowers: the form or colour of these flowers may be hidden from our eyes, but the fragrance tells us that there are flowers. So thoughts imply objects. The mind is like a mirror. Images in the mirror imply that there are objects before the mirror. Whether the mirror likes it or no, these are reflected in it. On the other hand, the mirror has not life; but the mind has. The mirror cannot create images, it can only reflect; but the mind has also innate ideas. In other respects, the mind is like a mirror, in that in it are reflected ideas of things outside, sometimes without the mind itself participating in the reflection. Abstract ideas are the sparks which come out from the fire of Reality.

3. The reflections in our mind do not always correspond to the Reality. They may appear different to different people according to their different capacities. Our ideas of God now are imperfect. But by living constantly in His Presence, we shall attain to a real understanding of His Being.

9
PHILOSOPHY AND INTUITION

It is admitted that for centuries Philosophy has made no advance. The same old problems and the same old solutions are repeated, though in new forms and new words. A blindfolded ox in India goes round and round an oil press all day long. When, in the evening, his eyes are opened, he finds that he has only moved round in a circle and has not travelled far, though he has produced some oil. Though philosophers have travelled for centuries, they have not yet reached their goal. Out of the material they have gathered here and there, they have produced some oil which they have left behind in their books. But this oil is not enough to remove the dryness of human needs. To go further is the work of faith and intuition, not of philosophy. However vast our knowledge may be, it has, after all, its limits.

2. Some philosophers committed suicide when the thirst of their knowledge was not quenched. Empedocles threw himself down into the crater of Etna in order to quench his thirst for knowledge by attaining the fellowship of the gods without dying a natural death. An astronomer who failed to understand the strange movements of the tides threw himself in despair into the billows and sought a watery grave. Such men, instead of finding the Creator in His creation and being satisfied in Him, lost the Creator as well as themselves, in His creation. This shows that though philosophy sets out to understand Reality, it fails; no one can grasp Reality by the intellect. If any one thinks that he can discern Reality by his knowledge, he is mistaken. For to know one thing thoroughly would be to know the whole universe, as any one thing is related to every thing else,

and to know all about it, all its relations need to be known. Here we have to bow before Reality and to walk along in faith.

3. Intuition, like the tip of a finger, is so sensitive that it at once feels the presence of Reality by its touch. It may not be able to give logical proof, but argues thus: I am fully content. Such peace can only come from Reality. Therefore I have found Reality. The heart has reasons of which the head knows nothing. It takes a long time to know much about a flower. But it takes but a moment to enjoy its fragrance. Intuition also works thus.

10
PERFECTION

According to the laws of Nature, it is necessary to grow gradually by stages in order to attain perfection. In this way alone can we make ourselves ready and fit for the destiny for which we have been created. Sudden or hurried progress leaves us weak and imperfect. The oats which grow in a few weeks in Lapland do not yield the same nourishment as the wheat which takes six months to ripen. The bamboo grows three feet daily and shoots up one hundred and eighty five feet, but it remains empty and hollow within. Slow and gradual progress, therefore, is necessary for perfection.

2. It is true that perfection can be attained only in a perfect environment. But before entering the perfect environment we have to pass through an imperfect environment, where we have to make effort and struggle. This struggle makes us strong and ready for the perfect environment, just as the silkworm's struggle in the cocoon enables it to emerge out of it as a beautiful butterfly. When we reach the perfect state, we shall see how these things which seem to have hindered us have really helped us, though mysteriously, to reach perfection.

3. In man, there are seeds of countless qualities which cannot develop in this world because the means here are not conducive towards their growth and development towards perfection. In the world to come they will find the environment necessary for the attainment of perfection. But the growth must begin here. It is, however, too early to say in detail what we shall be when we reach perfection. But we shall be perfect, even as our Father which is in heaven is perfect (Matt. v. 48).

4. There is no real peace in this world. On

account of sin, peace in this world is shattered. Real and permanent peace is to be found only in the " Prince of Peace." Water flows down from heights or gushes up from depths to find its level and to attain calm. Just so man must come down from the heights of his pride and rise up from the depths of his sin, in order that, by reaching his level, he may rest in peace and calm.

5. On the Mount of Transfiguration, the disciples, even though they had not yet attained perfection, enjoyed so much the company of our Lord and of Elijah and Moses that they wanted to make three tabernacles and dwell there (Matt. xvii. 3, 4). How much more shall we, when we are perfect, enjoy the fellowship of our Lord and of His saints and angels in heaven for ever!

11
REAL PROGRESS AND SUCCESS

If people adopt the external manners and ways of living of civilised nations, without accepting the fundamental principles through which they make progress, the outcome will be destructive.

The governments of this world are but copies of the heavenly government of which God is the King. Therefore the governments of this world are likely to decrease and decay unless God, who is the Source of all Goodness and Order, rules in the hearts of administrators and citizens, of the rulers and the ruled. Some want to lead a moral life without God, but they forget that all morals without God are hollow and dead.

2. Without spiritual progress, worldly progress is sham and false, as worldly progress is not attained without loss to others. Men run in a race, but one wins by out-stripping the others. Their defeat becomes his victory. One merchant makes his fortune at the expense of others. On the other hand, spiritual progress is real, because one man's progress helps and depends on the success of others. Experience proves that one who works for the good of others is being helped himself, often without his own knowledge.

12
THE CROSS

Whether we like it or no, we cannot escape the cross. If we do not bear the cross of Christ, we would have to bear the cross of the world. At first the cross of Christ may seem heavy and the cross of the world light; but experience shows that, as a matter of fact, the cross of the world is heavy and the outcome of taking it up is the death of a slave, as in the days of the Roman Empire. But Christ has changed His cross into glory. Formerly the cross was a symbol of disgrace and death; now it denotes victory and life. Those who bear the cross know from experience that the cross bears them and takes them safely to their destiny. But the cross of this world drags us down and leads us to destruction. Which cross have you taken up? Pause and consider.

2. The cross is different with different people, according to their work and spiritual condition. Outwardly it may appear full of nails, but in its nature it is sweet and peaceful. The honey bee has a sting, yet it produces sweet honey. For fear of the outward difficulties of the cross, we must not lose its great spiritual blessings.

3. An ignorant traveller, tired of walking up and down mountains, might think that God had made a mistake in creating mountains and that it would have been much better if He had made only the plains. This means that he is not aware of the many uses of mountains and of the riches stored in them. For one thing, the mountains keep the water in circulation, and the circulation of water in the world is just as necessary as the circulation of blood in the body. In the same manner, the ups and downs of life and the hardships of bearing the cross

keep our spiritual life in circulation, prevent it from stagnation, and bring to the soul countless blessings.

4. During the Great War, trenches were dug in a fertile spot and fields were destroyed. In these trenches beautiful flowers and fruits began to appear after a time. It was discovered that the soil was fertile, under the soil there was earth which was still more fertile. So when we bear the cross and suffer, the hidden riches of our soul come to light. We must not despair of what appears to be a destructive process, for it sets the hidden, unused powers of our soul to work.

5. In Switzerland, a shepherd broke the leg of a sheep. When asked why he had done so, he said that she had the bad habit of leading other sheep astray and taking them to dangerous heights and precipices. The sheep was so angry that when the shepherd came to feed her she sometimes tried to bite him. But after a time she became friendly and would lick his hands. Just so, through sorrow and suffering, God leads those who have been disobedient

and rebellious to the path of safety and eternal life.

6. When cold, every gas absorbs some rays of light, when hot it emits them. Just so, when we are spiritually cold, we live in darkness, although the Sun of Righteousness is perpetually shining around us. But when the fire of the Holy Spirit is kindled in us by the friction of the cross and warmth is produced, then by His rays we are first enlightened ourselves and we carry the light to others.

7. Diamonds do not dazzle with beauty unless they are cut. When cut, the rays of the Sun fall on them and make them shine with wonderful colours. So when we are cut into shape by the cross we shall shine as jewels in the Kingdom of God.

13
FREE WILL

We have the capacity to discern the difference between good and evil, and to choose either. That means, we are free to act according to the limits of our being. Otherwise the power which we have of discerning between good and evil would have no meaning. The sense of taste tells us what is bitter and what is sweet. If we were not free to eat what we choose, this sense of taste would have no meaning. We are free, not because we might have acted otherwise, but simply because we act.

If I have, for instance, the strength to carry

a hundred pounds, then I am free to carry the whole or part of it. And if a burden is more than a hundred pounds it is beyond my power and also beyond my responsibility: then I am free from the necessity of carrying the burden, because he who has placed the burden on me will not require of me more than I can do. Therefore there is freedom in either case. And if I do not do something which is within the limits of my power, then I have to suffer for my shortcoming and indifference, because I have misused the power which has been given to me.

2. Evil and crime cannot be wiped out by punishing the criminal. If this could be done, all prisons would have to be closed. In spite of the severe punishment meted out to wrongdoers, we do not find any change. And neither is it possible to remove evil from the face of the earth until each man resolves by his own free will to wipe it out to the full extent of his capacity. Compulsion from others produces no effect. God does not catch the hand of the murderer or close the lips of the liar, because He

does not interfere with man's free will. If God did so, man would be like a machine; nor will he appreciate the Truth and find joy in acting according to it; since joy can only be the outcome of an act of free will.

3. The world which is, in a way, rebellious from God makes slaves of those who follow Christ. When by the grace of God they are set free from the bondage and control of the world's power and enter into heavenly places, then the world itself becomes their slave, because the world recognises that they have come into relationship with that living Power who has created it. Then, instead of overcoming, it is overcome. God grants a perfect freedom for ever to those who serve Him with love of their own free will.

14
RULES OF HEALTH

Principles of health, physical and spiritual, are themselves means to health. Principles are nothing else than the appointed means by which special object might be attained. Money, for instance, is of no use in itself. It is only a means to obtain the things we need. Music, fragrance, dainty food, light and warmth — these we can enjoy if we have them in moderation. We feel the loss if there is not enough of them ; if there is more than enough, then do we suffer, God has given us senses, external and internal, so that they may warn us of impending dangers or indicate to us real happiness. Pain is the symptom showing that something is wrong in our body or mind. Rest and happiness are the outcome of obedience to the laws of Reality.

2. Nature is against us, if we are against her; but if we seek to live in conformity with Nature, then, instead of doing us harm, she will help us to reach that destiny of perfect health which God meant we should reach through these means. And in attaining perfect health we shall attain the eternal happiness in God, which is the primary longing of our soul.

15
CONSCIENCE

Conscience is the moral law or sense in us. It is not innate in personality, except in germ. It stands in need of education, training, exercise and habit. Environment also has great influence on its growth.

As we have an aesthetic faculty which enables us to distinguish between the ugly and the beautiful, so we have conscience which helps us to distinguish between good and evil.

2. Pain in any organ of the body is a voice which gives the alarm of danger. Just so, pain and unrest of soul are the result of sin. Like the sense of touch in the body, conscience warns

us of coming danger and destruction, and urges us to take the steps necessary for salvation.

3. Ships near the coast know where they are by seeing the lighthouse or the rocks or the outlines of the land. But those far out in the deep can be guided only by the stars and a compass. So in the voyage of our soul to God, conscience and the Holy Ghost are most necessary so that we should reach our destiny without going astray.

16
THE WORSHIP OF GOD

You will hardly find men who do not worship God or some Power, If atheistic thinkers or scientists, filled with the materialistic outlook, do not worship God, they often tend to worship great men and heroes or some ideal which they have exalted into a Power. Buddha did not teach anything about God. The result was, his followers began to worship him. In China the people began to worship ancestors, as they were not taught to worship God. Even illiterate people are found worshipping some Power or some spirit. In short, men cannot but worship. This desire for worship, from which man cannot get away, has been created in him by the Creator, so that, led by this desire, he may have communion with his Creator or enjoy eternal fellowship with Him.

2. And those who because of stubbornness do not believe in God, even though arguments for His existence based on design and order are placed before them, will not believe in Him even if they see Him. This for two reasons. If God reveals Himself to them and gives them reasons for proving His Godhead, reasons based on divine logic, they will not be able to understand Him, as such reasons will be far above the reach of their human logic and philosophy. If, on the other hand, He gives reasons following the canons of human knowledge, then too they will despise Him, saying, " Of course, we know all these. God is not much better than us, as His way of thinking seems to be only like ours. He may be a little higher than a human being, but no more."

3. Man is a part of the Universe and is a mirror reflecting it. Therefore creation, seen and unseen, is imaged in him. In this world, he

is the only being who can interpret creation. He is, so to speak, the language of Nature. Nature speaks, but silently. Man puts into words these silent utterances of Nature.

4. Man is a limited being; hence his senses, inner and outer, are also limited. Therefore he cannot perceive all the aspects of the Creator's creation. To know them all, he requires innumerable senses. Our few senses can perceive but few aspects of creation and its nature, and those not fully. In spite of these limitations, the heart has a conception of Reality which is independent of the intellect and whose aptness cannot be understood by the intellect. The human eye, though small in itself, sweeps over immense distances and reaches places where man himself cannot go. It beholds the stars, which are millions of miles away, observes their movements and enjoys their lustre. Just so the eyes of the heart gaze on the deep things of God, and this insight urges man to worship Him, in whom only he has the needs of his heart satisfied perfectly for ever.

17
THE SEARCH AFTER REALITY

Wise men from the East, coming from a far country, were led by the star to the Sun of Righteousness. These men who came from far away realised the desire of their hearts by seeing and worshipping the King of Righteousness, while in a sense His own people, the Jews, rejected and crucified Him and lost their blessing. People from East and West come to Him searching for Reality, and, finding Him, worship Him with heart and soul and lay themselves in sacrifice at His feet. By this sacrifice they inherit eternal life in His Kingdom. Christians, on the other hand, who are in a sense His own people, reject Him by word and deed and surfer untold loss. The wise men from the East did not stay long enough to hear the teaching of Christ and to see His miracles, His crucifixion, His resurrection and ascension, and therefore they did not have any message for the world. In the same way some seekers after Reality do not live in blissful fellowship with the Lord and experience His life- giving and saving power; so they have no message for the world.

2. "Unto every one that hath shall be given, and he shall have abundance; but from him that hath not shall be taken away even that which he hath" (Matt. xxv. 29). If a man has not, how can anything be taken away from him? He may not have any talents or responsible work as these have been taken away from him because of his negligence, but there has been left to him at least his capacity to distinguish between the real and the unreal. Even this power of discernment is taken away from him because he does not use it. After that, his conscience becomes numb and dead. Nothing is left to him.

3. There are some, whose power of discernment is so dead, that when they fail with their delicate scientific instruments to trace out the beginnings of life in this world, then, instead of believing in God as the source of all Life, they begin to think that germs of life fell down from meteors — surely an impossibility. If the dead matter of the world cannot produce life, how can meteors, made of the same kind of matter as the world, give rise to life? If matter in the meteors is different from matter on this earth, then how can germs from meteors grow in this world, where the environment is so different? The truth is, where there is God's Presence, there is Life. In water, whether hot or frozen, there are living insects. In hot springs, living creatures are found. This is the result of God's creative presence everywhere. He creates life under all conditions.

4. Truth or Reality is known by its fruits. He who acts in accordance with Reality enjoys, while thus acting, the fruits as well as in the future the ultimate good of habits. Reality alone can satisfy the craving of the soul.

A man, however fallen into sin and degraded he may be, likes and appreciates Truth. A liar, for instance, may tell lies himself, but he does not like that other people should tell lies. Another man, however unjust he may be himself, is annoyed if other people are unjust. This means that unconsciously there is in their natures a desire for and an appreciation of Truth and Justice, because it is Truth who has created them so that they might enjoy bliss by living for and in Truth. If they act against Truth, they shall suffer, because it is against their nature as well as against the nature of the Truth who has created them.

5. Truth has many aspects. Every one, according to his God-given capacity, reveals or gives expression to, different aspects of Truth. A tree may appeal to one man because of its fruits; to another because of its pretty flowers. Men appreciate and explain those aspects of the tree which appeal to them. So the philosopher, the scientist, the poet, the painter, and the mystic, each according to his capacity and temperament, will define and describe the different

aspects of Reality by which they have been influenced. It is not possible for one man to have an all-embracing view of Reality and to describe all its different phases.

6. We have to look at a thing from different sides to find out whether it is true or not. Otherwise misunderstanding and error will arise. When we look, for instance, with one eye at a straight stick from one of its ends, we have no idea of the length of the stick. In order to get a right idea of the stick, we have to see it from different sides.

He who searches for Reality with his whole mind and soul and attains it, realises that before he began to search for Reality, Reality itself had been searching for him to bring him into its blissful fellowship and presence; just as a lost child, seeking for his mother, realises, after getting into her lap, that she had begun searching for him with deep motherly love even before he thought of her.

18
REPENTANCE AND SALVATION

Repentance is necessary for salvation, but repentance alone cannot save sinners unless their sins are also forgiven by the grace of God. If I hurl a stone at a man and he dies and I repent, such repentance may prevent me from repeating the folly in the future, but the harm that has been done cannot be undone and the life of the man cannot be brought back. God alone can forgive me and give an opportunity to the dead man to make up in the next life the loss sustained by him by his sudden death. In this way, both the murderer and the murdered may be saved.

2. It is God alone who can punish or forgive rightly, because He alone understands the inner needs and conditions of man and knows what will be the outcome of his forgiveness or punishment. If man punishes, the purpose of punishment is not often attained, because he does not know the inner need and conditions of the wrongdoer. In some cases punishment will do harm, instead of good; whereas forgiveness has an almost magical effect in changing them. In the case of others, forgiveness may mean more opportunities for wrongdoing; punishment is necessary to reform such men. God alone knows the real nature of men and, according to their needs, saves them from the causes as well as the consequences of sin.

3. To obtain real and permanent joy is the aim of the soul. Any attempt to attain this aim by wrong means, such as sin, is destructive of the very capacity of the soul to enjoy happiness; and neglect and disuse of the capacity to enjoy results in its destruction. For God, who in His love has created in us these powers, capacities or senses for enjoyment, desires that in

fellowship with Him we might enjoy eternal happiness. This is salvation.

4. Pride is sin, because the proud man thinks of himself as being more than what he really is. By doing so, he loses the grace of God and, falling into sin, destroys his soul. Falsehood is sin, because it is spoken gainst the Truth. Gradually, the influence of constant falsehood on a liar is such that he begins to tell lies to himself. He ceases to trust in his own inner and outer senses, always doubting their truth. At last he begins to doubt even the love and grace of God and loses his spiritual life and God's richest blessings. Covetousness is sin because the covetous man seeks satisfaction in created things by forsaking the Creator. Adultery is sin, because the adulterer breaks family ties and destroys purity and life. Theft is sin, because the thief snatches away from others their earnings. He seeks joy in the loss of others. Therefore it is necessary that from these and all other sins we should repent and obtain salvation so that God's will might be

done in our lives on earth as it is done in heaven among saints and angels.

5. Scientists and philosophers who believe in evolution speak of the survival of the fittest by natural selection. There is, however, another greater fact, proved by the changed lives of millions, that in divine selection there is the survival of the unfit (i.e. sinners). Drunkards, adulterers, murderers, robbers, have been lifted up from depths of sin and misery and have received a new life of peace and joy. This is the salvation which is obtained through Jesus Christ, who came into the world to save sinners (1 Tim. i. 15).

19
ORIGINAL SIN

It is possible that children may inherit the diseases of parents. But if the parents lose hands, feet or eyes, then the children are not necessarily born lame, crippled or blind. So with original sin. Not all the qualities, good or bad, of the parents are inherited by the children; much of the children's character is the result of their own conscious acts. If they inherited all the qualities of their parents, then they could not be held responsible for their acts. Ability and character are inherited only in a small measure; their growth or maturity depends to a great extent on their own efforts.

2. If some object comes before light, it casts a shadow or produces darkness. The eclipse of the moon is caused by the earth coming between the sun and the moon. When the shadow of another object falls upon us, we are not responsible for it, since it is not we, but the external object, that has cast the shadow. As we are within the range of that shadow, we are affected by it, but we are not responsible for it. But we are responsible for the evil thoughts which rise from our hearts like clouds and float in the sky, causing darkness.

3. Sins and their consequences, though dangerous, are not external. Except God and those on whom He bestows eternity, nothing else is external. If another being were to exist by himself apart from God, he must also possess the infinite attributes which God has. That is impossible, because there is only One Absolute. God's existence is the guarantee of an ideal order that shall be permanently preserved. Anything opposed to His nature (i.e. evil) cannot exist in His presence for ever. Therefore

the whole creation which is groaning and in travail because of its subjection to evil and vanity shall be delivered for ever from the bondage of corruption into the glorious liberty of the children of God (Rom. viii. 20-22).

20
THE VEDANTA AND PANTHEISM

According to the Vedanta, God (Brahma) alone is real; everything else is an illusion. The human soul is the same as God, though on account of man's ignorance, it appears to be separate. If this be true, then it would mean that God also is subject to illusion. In that case, He cannot be God. God is really free from all illusion and knows everything. Vedantists also maintain that in deep contemplation {samadki), the devotee gets rid of illusion {may a) by means of knowledge. The question arises: If everything is illusion, how do we know that the devotee absorbed in samadhi and his knowledge derived from that state are not illusion?

2. If we admit the truth of the Vedanta, then we shall be obliged to admit that God also — man being identical with God — is in evolution, and that by means of illusion and changes of matter He wants to attain perfection. If maya does not do this for God, Vedantists must tell us what the first cause of maya is; as a result of what actions we are entangled in maya; and the purpose and ultimate good of maya. As a matter of fact, God is in everything and everything is in God. But God is not everything and everything is not God. Those who confound the Creator with His creation are sunk in ignorance.

21
CHRIST OUR REFUGE

A honey bee goes to a flower to gather honey. While engaged in this delightful task, it is sometimes stung by a spider. This sting makes it numb, and the bee falls an easy prey to the spider. Likewise, Satan may attack us not only in evil places, but also while we are engaged in doing good, useful and pleasant work. If we are not prayerful, there is a danger of our being attacked and overwhelmed by Satan.

2. On account of sin, the conscience becomes numb and the will is made weak and powerless. In such a condition, a man, seeing

death and danger ahead, is unable to escape them — so helpless is he — even though he has a strong desire to do so. Once in the depth of winter, a bird of prey sat on a corpse that was floating on towards the Niagara Falls and was busy feasting on it. When the bird came near the Falls, he wanted to leave the corpse and escape. But his claws were so frozen that he could not fly away, but fell into the roaring waters and died a miserable death.

3. To be safe from all attacks and dangers from the enemy, we must, by living in fellowship with the Lord, become like Him. In snowy countries, Nature clothes animals and birds in white so that they are of one colour with the surrounding environment and are thus secure from attacks. Where the environment is different, the animals are clothed in a different way. The chameleon and the bay flat-fish can change their colour in a moment and, assuming the same colour as that of the surrounding environment, escape from their enemies. Blind fish, however, cannot do so as they cannot see the colour around. In the same way, it is most

important to have spiritual vision so that by constantly gazing on Christ and following Him, we may become like Him, live in Him in safety for ever, protected from all attacks of the enemy.

22
ENEMIES BIG AND SMALL

Man's deadly enemies are not only big animals like tigers, wolves and snakes. Small germs which can only be seen through the microscope and which get into us through our food, water or air are often still more dangerous and cause fatal diseases. Just so, not only are great sins fatal to the soul, but hidden, evil thoughts, which are the germs of sins great and small, are even more destructive. We must try to remove these germs from the very outset from our minds so that we and others may be free from their fatal consequences.

2. In our body there are germs of health (phagocytes) as well as germs of disease (bacteria). If under any circumstances the germs of disease increase and overwhelm the germs of health, man falls ill and, if he is not treated properly, he dies. But if the germs of health are stronger, they resist and kill the germs of disease, and the man enjoys perfect health. Likewise our good thoughts overwhelm our evil thoughts and help us to enjoy sound health, free from the ravages of sin. This victory cannot be attained without the help of the Holy Spirit, who is the Source of all goodness, joy and perfect life.

3. Evil thoughts so overcome some men that they seem to lose all hope, and in great despair commit suicide. But instead of killing themselves, they ought rather, with the help of God, to kill those thoughts which kill their hopes and their capacity for victory. Instead of using poison or deadly weapons to put an end to our lives, we must use spiritual implements like prayer to destroy evil, root and all. Then we do not kill ourselves but save ourselves,

and in so doing help also others to save themselves.

4. Selfishness also is in a way suicide, for God has given us certain capacities and qualities so that we might use them for the benefit of others. In helping others we find a new joy and also help ourselves. This is a law of our inner being. If we do not help others, then we lose this joy. By not loving our neighbours as ourselves, we disobey God. Such disobedience deprives us of the joy which is the very food of our souls. By such starvation, we kill ourselves. A selfish man thinks that he is working for his gain, but unconsciously he is doing great harm to himself. If every one could only make up his or her mind to abandon selfishness, then all the quarrels and struggles in the world would cease and earth would become heaven. All sins arise from selfishness. That is why our Lord commanded us to deny self and to follow Him (Luke ix. 23).

5. If we constantly criticise and blame others, we do great harm both to them and ourselves. But if we abandon self- praise and

criticise ourselves, that will reform us and make us sympathetic and loving towards others. In this way, both others and we shall be benefited. And we shall inherit the promised land, which is the kingdom of real love.

23
"STRANGERS AND PILGRIMS ON THE EARTH"

A philosopher travelled around the world to find a place of perfect calm and rest. He found instead sin and sorrow, suffering and death everywhere. By the knowledge and experience so gained thus, he arrived at the conclusion that this world is not meant to be our permanent and real home; but that that real home, for which we have such deep longing in our soul, is elsewhere. There the soul will find perfect rest.

2. Once a bird was caught near the Gulf of Mexico and sent ofF to a place eight hundred and fifty miles away. It was put in a close cage

and did not know the way along which it was taken. But when it grew up, it returned without any guidance or help to the very same spot from which it had been taken away. Instinct did it. Just so, the man whose conscience is alive by the grace of God leaves this transitory world and, with the guidance and help of the Holy Spirit, reaches heaven, the eternal home for which he has been created.

3. A naturalist took the eggs of a nightingale to a cold country, and hoped that when hatched the birds would regard that country as their home and remain there. But they came out, and, after the summer, they flew away to their native home and never came back. Similarly, though born in this world, we are not for this world. As soon as the time comes for us to leave the body, we shall move away into our eternal home.

4. At the time of death the soul does not die, nor does it go away to some far-off place. But through death it begins a new life, entering a new state. As a child coming out from a mother's womb begins new life by entering

into a new state, but the world or place he lives in continues to be the same, so the spirit after coming out of the body enters into a far better spiritual state, although the world in which it lives continues to be the same. The child in the mother's womb and the spirit in the body remain in ignorance of their future condition, as that is hidden from their eyes. The child after coming out of the womb is unable to see the womb from which it came, and the soul after leaving the body, except under certain conditions, is unable to see the physical world from which it came, as it lives always in the spiritual world, and the physical world is but coarse matter enfolded in the spiritual. As by cutting the umbilical cord the child is severed from the mother's womb, so the spirit is severed from the body by cutting off the silver cord (Eccles. xii. 6). The mother's womb for the child, and the body for the soul, are places of preparation for the future. From the body the spirit passes into God's presence, where it attains its real destiny and perfection.

24
FAITH AND PURITY

Without faith, no work, whether spiritual or secular, can be done. If we did not believe in one another, life in the world would be impossible. When everything depends so much upon faith, what shame it is if we do not trust in Him who has created in our nature the capacity for faith! Of course, if our knowledge were infinite, there would be no need for faith; but when our knowledge is so limited that it is almost nothing, then in this world we shall always stand in need of faith. And indeed in the next world also, for even then our knowledge will not be infinite.

Faith, like love, is the tendril of the soul which clings to God, puts out branches and leaves and brings forth abundant spiritual fruit.

2. By faith we receive the baptism of the fire of the Holy Ghost. Without this, the baptism of water is not enough for purity and salvation. Silver and gold can be cleansed by water only on the outside, as it cannot penetrate into them to purify them. Fire is necessary to refine them. The baptism of the fire of the Holy Spirit is necessary to purify the soul completely.

25
REVELATIONS OF CHRIST

Without receiving the Holy Spirit, we cannot understand the greatness and Godhead of Christ, although we may follow Him all our life. This is clear from the experiences of the disciples. Christ called the disciples from a lower to a higher and nobler work, from being fishermen to be fishers of men. They lived three years with Him. During those years, they did the noble work of preaching to men the good tidings of salvation. But when Christ was crucified and buried, all their hopes were laid in His grave. The disciples went back again to do the same old work which they had been doing before for their living. But Christ, who they thought was dead, rose again from the dead and appeared to them on several occasions. Once when He appeared to His disciples by the Sea of Galilee Peter recognised Him as the Lord, and was so much ashamed that he jumped into the water to hide himself. For this there were most likely two reasons. One was that this was the first time he saw Christ after his denial, and he was ashamed, thinking: I declared solemnly that I would give up even my life for Christ and that I would not by any means deny Him. But I did deny Him. How can I now stand before Him? The other reason most probably was that he was ashamed when he realised that three years ago at that very spot he and the other disciples had been called to the great work of bringing men to Christ, and that after three years they had given up the nobler service and had gone back to the old work and were following it in the same place, while they should have continued the great work to which Christ had called them. When Christ rose from the dead, their dead hopes also came to life, and when further they received the fullness of the Holy Spirit, they realised anew the Godhead of Christ and continued to the end of their lives, in spite of persecution and martyrdom, to preach Him and to carry on the work for which they had been called.

2. At the present time there are many Christians who have been following Christ without experiencing His greatness and Godhead in their own, inner lives. So they have gone astray. They think that Christ was a great and perfect man who lived and died centuries ago. But to those who repent and pray, He reveals Himself again in His glory and powers as to St. Paul. They renew their fellowship with Him, and by the power of the Holy Ghost faithfully serve Him to the end of their lives.

26
HUMILITY

If the spirit of Christ does not dwell in us, we cannot be humble and meek like Him, who, being God, took upon Him the form of a servant (Phil. ii. 6, 7). We must not give room for false pride in our hearts, forgetting what we really are. By pride we shall fall away from Truth and destroy ourselves. Even though we have made more progress than other men, we must not forget that diamond and coal are made of the same substance, viz. carbon. Owing to different conditions they have taken such different forms, but a diamond, though so valuable, can be burnt away as completely as can coal.

2. When we stand on the edge of a precipice and look down we feel dizzy and are afraid, though the depth may be only a few hundred feet. But we are never afraid when we gaze at the heavens, though our eyes may range over much greater heights. Why? Because we cannot fall upwards. There is, however, a danger of falling down and being dashed to pieces. When we look up to God, we feel that we are safe in Him and that there is no danger whatever. But if we turn away our face from Him, we are filled with fear lest we fall down from Reality and be broken to pieces.

27
TIME AND ETERNITY

Real time, i.e. time in its relation to Reality, is eternity. Time as we know it is a passing shadow of that real time. For God there is no Past and Future, everything is Present. Being infinite in knowledge, the Past and the Future stand before Him. But for us the Present has no existence, as it is only a passing away of the Future into the Past. Every moment emerges from the Future and glides into the Past with unimaginable quickness. The Past and the Future also do not exist for us, as they are beyond our reach. Therefore Time has no reality for us. When we awake from sleep, we are hardly able to tell how much Time has passed during our sleep. Even in our waking moments, Time is so unreal. In sorrow and suffering, a day seems to be a year; in joy, a year a day. Time has no Reality, therefore, for Reality is real under all circumstances, and we have no sense for Time as we have been created for Reality, which is Eternal.

2. Year, month, day and hour, minute, second, create what we call Time by reference to incidents or changes of objects in space. Take any object in space; its change creates Time. When the change is taking place, it is Present; when the change has taken place, it is past; when the change is still to take place, it is Future. When objects change, Time also changes with them into Future or Past. On the other hand, Reality changes neither itself nor the eternity with which it is connected.

3. Time may change and be lost in oblivion. But whatever we have done in Time will never be wiped out, but pass into Eternity.

"The world passeth away, and the lust thereof; but he that doeth the will of God abideth for ever"

— I JOHN II. 17

THE END

Copyright © 2023 by FV Editions
Cover design and layout : FVE
Ebook ISBN 979-10-299-1514-7
Paperback ISBN 979-10-299-1515-4
All rights reserved.

Also Available

www.ingramcontent.com/pod-product-compliance
Lightning Source LLC
LaVergne TN
LVHW031607060526
838201LV00063B/4758